C.S. LEWIS

The Writer Who Found Joy

narrated by Gilbert the Owl

Daniel DeWitt

illustrated by Marcin Piwowarski

B&H kids
Brentwood TN

Dedicated to Addilynn Joy,
the girl who stole her father's heart.

COAST OF IRELAND

Can you find 20 lions inside this book? Look carefully from page 1 to 32—they are many shapes and sizes!

Text copyright © 2023 by Daniel DeWitt
Art copyright © 2023 by B&H Publishing Group
Published by B&H Publishing Group, Brentwood, Tennessee
All rights reserved.
978-1-0877-5923-4
Dewey Decimal Classification: CB
Subject Heading: LEWIS, CLIVE STAPLES \ JOY AND SORROW \ CHRISTIAN LIFE
Printed in Dongguan, Guangdong, China, January 2023
1 2 3 4 5 6 • 27 26 25 24 23

Greetings!

I'm Gilbert the Owl. I get to tell you a story about a writer who spent half his life looking for joy and the other half telling the world about the joy he found in God.

Once upon a time, in a faraway land filled with green hills, craggy cliffs, and shiny seashores, there was a boy who lost his mom.

The boy's name was Clive Staples Lewis, but
he didn't like his name all that much. When the
neighborhood dog Jacksie died, Clive took that
name for himself. He later shortened it to Jack,
which is what most of his friends called him.

Jack grew up with a big brother named Warnie and a dad named Albert. He lived in a huge house filled with long hallways, loads of books, and an old wardrobe made by his grandfather.

Jack's grandfather carved the wardrobe's wood and made the very nails that held it together. No wonder Jack never forgot it. He even used the wardrobe to tell an amazing story about four children who found a magical land. I'll get to that in a bit.

Jack loved to play and use his imagination.
The wonder of the world amazed him, but
he felt like he was missing something.

TOY GARDEN

He wasn't sure what to think about God. Could he trust Him? After Jack lost his mom to cancer, much of his life seemed sad and quit making sense. But it didn't stop him from looking— and hoping—to find true joy.

As a teenager, Jack didn't go to school with other boys and girls. He had a private teacher. He loved learning and ate up knowledge like you might **gobble up** candy on the last day of October.

Like Jack, his teacher had a nickname: "the Great Knock." The teacher didn't believe in God, which was okay since Jack had stopped believing too. But joy still called to him, kind of like a phone ringing when no one answers it. Joy refused to leave Jack alone.

Jack studied great books, different languages, and even how to think about thinking. That sounds strange, doesn't it? But one subject was never easy for him—math.

Jack's love of learning led him to England to study
in the city of one of the oldest schools in the world:
the University of Oxford.

He was excited to begin the life he had dreamed of,
one filled with books and laughter and knowledge.
Maybe now he would find true joy.

But it was not to be. A great war broke out all around the world, and Jack left college to become a soldier.

RIEZ-DU-VINAGE, FRANCE

He saw many sad and scary things. He lost a lot of friends in the war, including his best friend, Paddy. Jack was injured too. Joy seemed so very far away now.

Jack promised Paddy he would take care of Paddy's mom if anything happened to him. Jack kept that promise. After returning from war, Jack took care of Paddy's mother for years and years.

After the war, Jack finished college and became a professor. As he taught others, he kept learning, and he kept asking big questions: *Was God real? Could he trust God? Where could he find joy?*

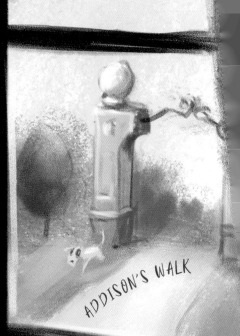

These questions were like a stray dog that followed Jack everywhere he went.

ADDISON'S WALK

Questions popped into Jack's thoughts like popcorn. They popped up in books he read. They even popped up in conversations with friends—like the time Jack went for a late-night walk with his good friend J.R.R. Tolkien, who was a Christian. They talked about God for hours.

You might have heard of J.R.R. Tolkien. He wrote famous stories, too, although his were about happy hobbits and a smelly dragon.

Their conversation made Jack think harder than he had thought in all his life. He couldn't deny it any longer. This young man who had lost faith in God as a child had found it again. He didn't have all the answers, but he knew one thing for certain:

he believed in God.

So he prayed and told God all about it.

Jack believed in God, but he didn't decide to follow Jesus until the morning he took a motorcycle ride to the zoo with his brother. When they began the ride, Jack wasn't sure about Jesus. By the time they arrived at the zoo, he somehow knew Jesus was God's Son, sent to forgive the sins of the world.

What happened on the ride, you ask? That's a good question. The answer is, God had done a mighty work in Jack's heart.

SIDECAR

C.S. Lewis, whose friends still knew him as Jack, was surprised by joy—God's joy. He wanted to share his happiness with the whole world, so he talked on the radio, wrote books, taught students, and even used stories about talking animals to speak of God's love.

In his third science-fiction book, C.S. Lewis introduced a bear who defeats the bad guy. The bear, **Mr. Bultitude**, was based on a bear at the zoo!

C.S. Lewis celebrated his newfound joy with his friends. They called themselves **the Inklings** and often met at a place called The Eagle and Child to share their writing with each other. But as they laughed and enjoyed their time together, another world war began.

Members of the Inklings came and went, but C.S. Lewis and J.R.R. Tolkien stayed. The books they read to each other are still loved by hundreds of thousands of readers around the world.

EAGLE AND CHILD

A man named Hitler, whom you might have heard of, was trying to take over the world. He began bombing London, not far from where C.S. Lewis lived. Families sent their children to live safely away from the city. Some children even stayed in Lewis's home.

As the bombs fell, Lewis's main concern wasn't his safety. He wanted to tell the world about the joy he had found in God. So he took a train to London—right where the danger was!—to talk on the radio about God's love.

He later turned his talks into a book called *Mere Christianity*, which has helped countless readers believe in God.

C.S. Lewis wrote a lot of books to share his faith. Some of the most popular ones were for children: *The Chronicles of Narnia*. The stories tell about four siblings who left London during the war.

Their adventures begin when they enter a wardrobe and discover a magical world. There they meet a talking faun named Mr. Tumnus, some very polite beavers, a brave mouse, and, most importantly, a mighty lion named **Aslan**.

Does that wardrobe remind you of anything? Stories often give us pictures of writers' real lives. The children who found Narnia were much like those staying at C.S. Lewis's house during the war. And the beloved Aslan is a picture of how much the writer loved Jesus.

One day, C.S. Lewis received a letter from a woman in America. You won't believe her name—Joy! The two met in person, fell in love, and got married.

Joy was a gifted writer too. She and her two sons all moved to the "Kilns," the nickname C.S. Lewis gave their home. They lived happily together as a family.

SNIP THE CAT

SUSIE THE DOG

Sadly, their happiness didn't last very long. Just a few years into their marriage, Joy died from cancer.

But C.S. Lewis didn't stop believing in God like he had after his mother died of cancer so many years before. He clung even more tightly to his belief, like you might cling to a blanket, a stuffed animal, or a parent when you're troubled at night.

Through good times and bad,
C.S. Lewis had learned to trust
God. His belief helped him make
sense of the world. It showed
him how to find joy even when
he felt stuck in sadness.

On a cool November day in 1963, C.S. Lewis took his final breath. I like to imagine that if you were walking around Oxford that day and listening closely,

you might have heard a lion roar.

C.S. Lewis found joy by finding God. He was a truly happy Christian. And I have no doubt—he would want you to know you can find joy in God too.

Surprised
by
JOY